"*Kiss of God* is a beautiful, profound work. . . . Oh Marshall—what a gift you are and what a gift you have given in *Kiss of God*."

—Diana Bort
midwife, Boston, Massachusetts

"God has given you a wonderful gift and it is clearly apparent in your writing you know that, too. I work every day with people, well-educated people, who cannot express themselves like you. It is so much more that you have chosen to express yourself with love and in loving ways."

—Ben Turner
engineer, Austin, Texas

"The love and joy portrayed in Marshall's thoughts have had a profound impact on me. . . . Let him know that one more person thinks of him daily."

—Suzanne Fairlie
career placement business owner, Ambler, Pennsylvania

"God has provided you with a loving touch. He also has gifted you as an encourager. As I read your poetry I am forced to stop and listen. For that I thank you because it is hard to stop doing all these important things that are really not very important."

—Marks Gilliam
publisher, Austin, Texas

"Marshall, you took my heart and gave it a home—within me. Thank you."

—Jo Ogden
mother, Houston, Texas

"You are a maestro to this wonderful symphony of love, and that is why I refer to you as Maestro Marshall."

—William H. Webster Jr.
video producer, St. Louis, Missouri

"How can any of us take life or the world for granted after seeing it anew through your eyes."

—John Andrews
state senator, Denver, Colorado

"I am so pleased that you allowed us to share your wonderful, thoughtful and delight-filled insight with the world."

—Richard Halpin
executive director
American Institute for Learning, Austin, Texas

"Kiss of God" is so extraordinary—I return again and again to it. A beautiful book in every way, and what a spirit!"

—David Mallery
director of professional development
National Association of Independent Schools

"Marshall reminds me of that verse from scripture which says, 'The love of God constrains us.' To constrain means to push in on all sides in order to propel something forward. God has pushed Marshall and me in on all sides but, oh, the gifts which have been advanced forward!"

—Joni Eareckson Tada
JAF Ministries

Kiss of God

The Wisdom of a
Silent Child

Marshall Stewart Ball

Health Communications, Inc.
Deerfield Beach, Florida

www.hci-online.com
www.marshallball.com

Library of Congress Cataloging-in-Publication Data

Ball, Marshall Stewart, 1986-

Kiss of God: the wisdom of a silent child / Marshall Stewart Ball.

p. cm.

ISBN 1-55874-743-5 (pbk.)

1. Developmentally disabled children Poetry. 2. Children's writings, American. 3. Religious poetry, American. 4. Aphorisms and apothegms. I. Title

PS3552.A45537K5 1999

811'.54—dc21

99-41265

CIP

ISBN 1-55874-743-5

Publisher: Health Communications, Inc.
           3201 S.W. 15th Street
           Deerfield Beach, FL 33442-8190

Cover design by Larissa Hise
Inside book design by Dawn Grove

Caring Marshall dedicates this book to
Marshall's good candid teacher, Good God.

Mearwild
October 1998

Great kisses are loving,
grand, great little thoughts.

Foreword

Seeing Beneath and Beyond
Experiencing the Wonder
of Marshall Ball

I was gently introduced to Marshall by his parents, Charlie and Troy Ball, some two years before I actually met him in person. Looking back, my preparation had been slow and deliberate. I was being most carefully prepared to encounter, to appreciate this extraordinary being. I was being made ready to receive the gift.

In 1990, when Scottish autistic-savant artist Richard Wawro came to Texas for an exhibition, I was approached by a young couple who wanted to purchase an original drawing of horses for their three-and-a-half-year-old son who did not speak and had other (unnamed) developmental characteristics. I remember,

at the time, being struck by the intense glow and profound peace surrounding this young couple, and by
their extremely positive and joyful acceptance of this
special child who had been given to them as their
firstborn. I sensed the gentleness and strong love that
flowed through this couple toward their son.

It was not until two years later in late September
1992 when I visited at Duane Lake Academy, a home
school, that I met a young boy sitting on his mother's
lap being taught pre-algebra by a brilliant engineer
and mathematician, Dr. Neil Lubart. I was at first
somewhat skeptical as I saw this child of six-and-a-
half seem to communicate by pointing his fingers
slowly at the two-and-a-half-inch block letters on a
handmade alphabet board. As he pointed (his elbow
was supported to provide a fulcrum for the movement
of his hand), someone transcribed each letter that was
pointed to. It was a slow, laborious process. I discovered that the child was Marshall Ball. Clearly much
had happened since I had first met his parents in
1990.

As I came to know him and to experience some of
his capabilities and insights, I began to share a wider
range of thoughtful literature with him: *The Little
Prince* by Antoine de Saint-Exupéry, *Mister God, This
Is Anna* by Anna Fynn, *What Men Live By* by Leo

Tolstoy, *God's Trombones* by James Weldon Johnson, *The Hound of Heaven* by Francis Thompson, and many others.

On October 1, 1992, I transcribed the first of several pieces of Marshall's writing. Marshall titled his piece "My Harmony Prevails to Free." As one letter followed another, my eyes became wider and wider and my amazement and awe grew greater. What began to emerge from Marshall's pointing was:

> Even though my individuality finds
> sweet knowing perfection, I listen
> for the answers to wishes from above.

Only a week later Marshall surprised his mother one afternoon by writing through his board that he wanted her to purchase him a Bach compact disc. She didn't know that he even knew who Bach was. After listening to the CD, he wrote "Remember Rooms Rest" which includes the astonishing line,

> I listening marvelously, juxtaposed in
> wonderment, finding solitude near.

Marshall was six-and-a-half years old!

Little did I know that his mother had been carefully collecting these gemstones of wisdom for years. She had several, three-inch thick, loose-leaf notebooks filled with his writings. As I realized the significance of this treasure, I urged her to begin to share Marshall's insights with a larger audience. I was already scheduled to have an exhibition of the art of Richard Wawro during the annual conference of the Texas Association of Gifted and Talented to be held in Austin. Some five thousand parents, teachers and educators were to attend. I suggested that his mother select several of his writings to print on cards and make them available for sale during the conference.

During the three-day conference Marshall joined me in the booth, talking to people through his alphabet board and selling several hundred cards.

In 1996 Marshall wrote and published "That Fine Example" for a national literary competition on the subject "What America Means to Me." In it he poses the powerful question:

Can willful Americans begin to answer
happily, lovingly, interestingly
that challenge finely given,
really carefully declared
by caring, listening, loving thinkers?

But for me, one of the most haunting and challenging questions he asks is found in "Free the World," the poem that concludes *Kiss of God*.

> Will we free the world to think perfectly
> about the listening
> and marvelous children?

As I have traveled throughout the country these past six years sharing Marshall's story and his writings, I have seen the impact his questions have had on countless individuals. They in turn have asked me questions: How did you discover his marvelous writing talent? How did it come about? First of all, I did not discover it. His parents were led over a period of time to discover his amazing insight and sensitivity. I am convinced that it came about primarily through the powerful and unconditional love of his family who refused to see him as incomplete in any way. They acted toward him as the perfect being they see him to be. They acted as though he were already the magnificent being he has come to be. Being ever totally present to him—seeing with the eyes of faith—beneath and beyond the surface to reach the seed of perfection lying within. As Ira Progoff so eloquently states in *The Symbolic and the Real*:

But this is one of the things that love is called upon to do: To affirm and sustain the seed in a fellow human being even though no tangible evidence has been given of the nature and quality of the seed that is growing there.

Love depends upon the capacity to reach beneath the surface of persons, to feel and touch the seed of life that is hidden there. And love becomes a power when it is capable of evoking that seed and drawing it forth from its hiding place. (pp. 165–166)

David Henry Feldman, in *Nature's Gambit,* an extraordinary book about child prodigies and the development of human potential, has described the unique response, the special environment that allows such rare talents as Marshall's to develop. I am convinced he captures the essence of the Balls' faith when he says of another family:

They both possessed an unusual willingness to act immediately on requests or other signs of interest, virtually regardless of time or place, and both sets of parents possessed an incredibly strong conviction— transmitted with great love, physical affection and even vehemence—that their child was extraordinarily special and wonderful. (p. 118)

The seed within Marshall Ball has indeed been drawn forth by the overwhelming power of love that daily surrounds him and *Kiss of God* bears witness to both his God-given talent and the love which nourishes it.

Laurence A. Becker, Ph.D.
mentor, student, friend
Creative Learning Environments
Austin, Texas
March 1999

Preface

Sharing Beyond Family and Friends
The Wonder of Marshall Ball

His Mother's Story

When the suggestion was made that I write about Marshall, I discussed the idea with him. He wrote, "You have my pleasing lovely world. Would you tell, my quiet roots would take us to Marshall's darling thoughtful teacher Good God?" I assured him I would and then asked if there was anything else he would want me to say. He asked me to take time to tell you "daring to marvelously upgrade our knowledge of lovely thinking, nicely pleases the heart. Poorly using man, pertaining to dear wisdom will heal nothing." And lastly, "Room is here to free." These three statements are pure Marshall. He is continually showing appreciation for his life, no matter how difficult it seems to others. His relationship with God is clear, and he challenges us to upgrade our thinking and treatment of all people, reminding us we can do these things now.

Marshall writes effortlessly, easily, though it may take minutes or hours to actually get his thoughts transcribed. He seems to always know what the next word is; there is never a delay in his thinking. I, on the other hand, struggle with the arrangement and choice of words. The idea of sharing his life with you without the use of my voice, or even my gestures, seems overwhelming. As I sit here, I am ardently aware of Marshall and what it is like for him to communicate so beautifully and effectively without the use of his voice.

At three and a half, Marshall communicated with us for the first time. He leaned forward and touched his forehead to a button on a toy that made a meow sound. When I asked him if he could do it again, he gladly repeated his performance. He went on to correctly identify all the animals on the toy. We knew for the first time that he was listening. The years of expecting and waiting had at last come to an end. Words cannot express the joy we felt that December day.

By the time Marshall was four and a half, we had in place an effective communication method that allowed him to make choices about everything. I remember my father saying, "It's not what Marshall has to learn [from you], but what you have to learn about him." How correct he was. Marshall was showing 100 percent accuracy in all his schoolwork, using his head to point to answers. He took more time to answer than the average child, but the results were remarkable.

At five years of age, when Marshall began using an alphabet board and pointing to letters to spell words, his ideas were much like they are now. He wrote "Altogether Lovely," a favorite of many people, and the first that spoke of God.

God is good and merciful
because He is also bright and intelligent.
Seeing, feeling all that is true.
Clearly He feels and listens to all our desires.
Clearly He has everybody's
dreams in mind.
I see a God altogether lovely.

Several weeks after Marshall wrote this poem, we learned that my brother, Wes, had given a copy to a friend. This friend was so impressed that he shared it with members of his church. As a result, "Altogether Lovely" was read from the pulpit before a congregation of five thousand people! This news came as a surprise and an indication of things to come. Our young son, Marshall Stewart Ball, who we were told may never be able to do anything, was touching people's lives and their hearts.

Having Marshall as a son has been a tremendous lesson in patience, humility and wonder. Charlie and I have experienced nearly every emotion possible in our life with Marshall. When he was very young we surrounded him with love, we cried often and we worried continuously. We often asked, "Why?" and soon learned, "Why is a whine." Despite our concerns, we decided to treat Marshall as a perfect child, like we would treat any other. We read to him for hours and hours, sang songs, went to the zoo and museums, played classical music, and kissed him hundreds of times a day. We refused to limit him in any way. For this behavior we were undoubtedly thought foolish by some. But our course was set, and wonders have continued to unfold each and every day.

There has never been any doubt in Marshall's mind about his mission in life. Since the beginning of his writing life at age five, continuing into his thirteenth year, he has been a "teacher."

> I see myself as a teacher
> that knows about God.
> Good thoughts come to me
> and they teach.

He wants all of us to learn to be better listeners, better thinkers, and simply better people. For many years Marshall has told me that he "listens." At times you can see him quietly looking off into the distance, eyes slightly raised, and he truly seems to be listening. Recently, he once again expressed what I believe is his very reason for being:

> Words greatly present lessons,
> oscillating finely bound,
> opening great rich kind room
> inside wonderful hearts.

So Marshall writes—to all of us—hoping to challenge us or "dare" us, as he is so fond of writing, to be better listeners, richer people, loving others.

Recently, as we were discussing all the possibilities of how *Kiss of God* could be arranged, we asked Marshall what his thoughts were. Marshall wrote,

"Knowledge carries beauty in good Marshall's thinking. Feel like attempting good fine force, badly splits *Kiss of God* apart." When asked, "What do you mean when you say force?" Marshall answered, "Forcing is giving good book great organization. . . . Can you give love by force?" Taken momentarily by surprise, we sat in awe, then laughed with the knowledge that Marshall was teaching us in his positive, beautiful way, even as we were trying to help him.

Such is life with Marshall. I know he will lead me, if I listen, to the right decisions and answers in life. When I first learned about publishing this book, I shared some of the difficulties and responsibilities of the process with Marshall. He had one comment; "*Kiss of God* justifies all arranging that needs to be made." Succinct and to the point, I had my answer. I knew I had to, at last, share him with the world.

Troylyn Ball

Acknowledgments

Marshall harmoniously thanks that old through feeling, great each day happily understood, giving love to listening good me.

And real definite thanks to Dad, freeing fine Marshall.

To lovely Mama, Marshall thanks you for teaching me to greatly love like I do.

To good Bill, that learning Cara and Trey have balance needed to care, teach, learn like you do.

Can learning evidence give listening care like my beautiful, great, grandmother?

Thank you sweet amazing Dad, fine Mother, teaching good Luke, magnificent joyous caring Coulton, good thoughtful Trish, wonderful happy thankful good Cindy, balanced Wes.

Tightly tuned Marshall knows Laurence kisses love.

Good Nan and Pops that Marshall loves you.

Lovely Mama would you take my thoughts purely to marvelous thinkers?

Author's Note

Questions nicely want good answers. With the giving happy help of my good family and magnificent friends, I dearly love to think about joyous balance excellently discovered in answers to old questions. Answers giving nice thought gain their dear freedom in wonderful thoughtful poetry. That marvelous good task teaches us to listen.

I hope to gather thinkers
to give them my thoughts about Love.
Love to clean their ideas.
That cleaning might loosen the love
in their hearts.
Good thinkers take LOVE to heart
like gold in the evening, wild sun.

On October 1, 1992, at Duane Lake Academy in Austin, Texas, I wrote down with pencil on paper each letter as Marshall Ball, a first-grader, slowly pointed to one letter at a time on his alphabet board. After the hour-long session, I typed the entire one page transcript that he titled "My Harmony Prevails to Free." During the hour I was confused, amazed, delighted and in awe of what I saw emerge from his mind through his fingers. The choice of words, the images and the ideas were unlike any six-year-old's choices that I had ever encountered. Several words (such as "messages," "individuality," "govern," "harmoniously" and "prevails") in the transcript were later underlined by Marshall's mother because this was the first occasion that he had used each of the words in a writing. The first line has become one of my favorites to quote as I share with new friends Marshall's extraordinary ability and his looking to God for his direction.

Laurence A. Becker, Ph.D.

My Harmony Prevails to Free

Even though my individuality finds sweet knowing perfection I listen for the answers to wishes from above. I listen to good thoughts like something cloudy over mountain tops. Fine messages clearly govern my thinking. Feelings grow harmoniously making Love possible. Harmony might justify every marvelous idea given to Love. The seeing Marshall hopes to free the hopeless. Dear harmony needs progress governing fine thinking that I feel. I see harmony as the final known answer.

"Dear and Sweet" was written in 1995 as a Christmas gift to Marshall's father, Charlie Ball.

Dear and Sweet

Loving you,
giving nearly all that makes me happy.
Baldly giving me great love,
listening generously,
longly gaining learning,
caring lovingly about me.
Gladly, I love to know,
dear and sweet
my good, good God
generously through you
taught me.

Marshall wrote this letter on March 29, 1995, on his last visit to see his adopted great-great-grandpa, who was recovering from an injury due to a fall. Marshall met the writer Ryerson Johnson and his wife Lois, whom he calls "Lovely," in Lubec, Maine, when Ryerson was ninety-one years old. They quickly became fast friends and pen pals. Over the next two years, a close relationship developed leading to a number of trips between Austin and Maine. Marshall's life has been greatly enhanced by knowing Grandpa and Lovely.

Great-Great-Grandpa,

My feeling is our thoughts
ran together for love.

I love you,
Marshall

These thoughts were written by Marshall to put inside Easter eggs on April 10, 1993, when Marshall was six-and-a-half years old as a good way for him to participate in the celebration.

Listen to God's thoughts.

Good finds the sweet giver.

This letter was written October 14, 1993 to Ryerson and Lovely, sharing Marshall's thoughts about meeting Marlo Morgan, the bestselling author of Mutant Message Down Under. *After their meeting, Ms. Morgan included Marshall in the acknowledgments of her hardcover book, along with Og Mandino, Dr. Wayne Dyer and Dr. Elisabeth Kübler-Ross. "All accomplished authors/ lecturers and real people. Thanks to young Marshall Ball for dedicating his life to being a teacher."*

Dear Great-Great-Grandpa and
  Lovely,

I think it is nice that you have clear
ideas needed to make you grow. We
have a good friend named Marlo
Morgan. She really is a good thinker.
She lived with the Aborigines in the
Outback of Australia. Nicely she told
me that love dearly comes to the pre-
defined. I think she thought I will go
understanding ideal thought. Will sand
from the desert enter you that way?
Good to have the love of Marlo. I love
you magnificent Grandpa and Lovely.

Marshall

God thinks being selfishly sick
is not the bent of needy man.

I have a dream of careful definition
bearing good love,
definitely greatly balanced with harmony,
caring how real people feel.

Nicely think of being a good Dad.
Know that I feel nice,
for each day good Marshall
realizes he gently has
a perfect Dad.

Days before Marshall's sixth birthday, he wrote a letter to Robbie, a woman who quickly became a friend, whom he met in an old-fashioned drug store, the kind with soda fountains, while visiting his grandmother Jaynan.

It was a very hot summer in Texas, as it always is, so when Marshall and his mother strolled each day by the town's pharmacy, they would drop in to cool off and have a soft drink. Each day, the same woman, Robbie, waited on them. She spoke kindly with Marshall's mother and inquired about Marshall as he sat in his wheelchair, but she never spoke directly to him, not at first anyway.

On the third day, as Marshall and his mother were getting ready to leave, it became apparent that Robbie was upset about something, so Marshall's mother asked if there was anything wrong. Robbie quite suddenly explained that her husband had unexpectedly died about three months before and that she was really struggling with his death. She felt very alone especially since they didn't have children, and she wasn't sure what was going to happen with her life. Marshall's mother expressed her sorrow to Robbie and was glad this stranger had trusted her enough to share her story. She told Robbie that Marshall loved to write and that he might have something to tell her if she would like to listen. Robbie looked at Marshall, who had sat silently through each of their visits and sipped his drinks through a straw. She wasn't sure what to say, so she expressed her thanks to Marshall's mother and said she would see them tomorrow.

The next day, Marshall and his mother arrived at the drug store and quenched their thirst, for the sun was intolerably hot. Robbie was happy to see them, but a little surprised when Marshall's mother asked if she wanted to hear what Marshall had to say. She said yes with uncertainty in her voice because she wasn't sure how this was going to take place. She had never seen Marshall communicate. To her surprise, Marshall's mother asked her to please get a pencil and paper so that she could write down what Marshall would spell. Meekly she sat down across from Marshall's mother, who now was holding Marshall on her lap facing the table. Marshall sat in front of an alphabet board that was about sixteen inches by twelve inches and he began to slowly point to letters on the board, creating beautiful words.

As he began by describing Heaven as a "lovely golden dream above," tears rolled down Robbie's cheek. She continued to transcribe each word Marshall spelled, transfixed by the message and its giver. When Marshall finished writing, Robbie said no one had touched her more than Marshall had and that God must have known she needed Marshall to come into her experience. Wiping away her tears, she told Marshall she was going to frame his letter and keep it by her bed.

Later in their conversation, Robbie said it was strange that Marshall had written about roses, and that they were her favorite flower. By some quirk of conversation, it was also discovered that Robbie and Marshall shared the same birthday, July 26. For several years thereafter, Marshall received a birthday card and letter from Robbie. In the first one, she wrote that she had framed the letter, and it stood on her bedside table. In the last, she told Marshall that she was very happy and had recently married someone that she loved very much.

July 20, 1992

Dear Robbie,

   There is a quiet lovely
golden dream above. Are you
there? Are you dreaming of
your perfect love? Roses smell
perfect and perhaps lovely
roses will quiet very sweetly,
your rightly justified thoughts.

Loving you,
Marshall S. Ball

"Victory" was written as a gift to Lovely (Lois Johnson) on March 28, 1995, while visiting her in Lubec, Maine.

Victory

Victory is here.
It gives us that room
to quietly title our thoughts.
To grow happily,
quiet understanding takes bald,
good, real thinking.

That sweet thinking
never attempts to arrange us.
That pure, meager, bald
sweet victory, easily loves.

*A few thoughts written to Marshall's Aunt Cindy on her
birthday, September 13, 1993.*

Dear Sweet Cindy,

Lovely music teaches that for dear Marshall good music has a healing effect. Clearly, I find Bach like the fine thought of God. Good music goes with nice Cindy. There is good music to teach fine, real meager, sweet, clear Cindy. I love you. That definitely will never change.

The Loving Marshall

On October 8, 1992, Marshall wrote to his mother and asked her to buy a Bach compact disc. This came as a great surprise to her because it was one of the first "things" he had ever asked for, and she didn't realize six-year-old Marshall knew of the composer Bach.

Although they did listen to some classical music at home, Marshall and his mother had never really discussed or read about individual arrangements or composers. To make certain she had understood him correctly, she asked him to spell what he wanted again. Once again he spelled "a Bach CD." Happy that Marshall had actually asked for something and that it was as wonderful as classical music, they planned an outing that afternoon.

When they arrived at the music store and saw the immense selection of J. S. Bach music available, they quickly sought the assistance of a store manager. He was very patient and waited for Marshall and his mother, who sat on the floor so Marshall could be held and use his communication board, to answer his questions about Marshall's favorite instruments. Marshall spelled that the violin was his favorite instrument. With this information, the manager narrowed the selection and eventually they left with Marshall's first CD in hand.

After returning home and feeling a little weary from the journey in the heat, Marshall's mother laid him down on a big bed covered in white, turned on the ceiling fan, and put his Bach CD on to play. While his mother was busy checking on Coulton, Marshall's younger brother, Marshall enjoyed the cool breeze and soft music.

When the CD ended, Marshall's mother asked him if there was anything he would like to do. He wrote "I want to write." So they sat down at a table together and Marshall began writing a poem. It began "The wind changes direction . . ." The poem took quite a long time for him to write because there were at least five words he had never used before including "lornfully," "juxtaposed," "wonderment," "solitude" and "sovereignty." When his mother asked him if he knew what "juxtaposed" meant, Marshall spelled "yes" and then gave her his definition which explained the word well. The word "lornfully" came from his imagination and understanding, conveying a sense of quiet sadness.

When asked what the title was, Marshall spelled

"Remember Rooms Rest," taking us back to the first time he listened knowingly to Bach, in a cool white room. In this poem, Marshall gave his mother a bold example of his understanding of and finesse with words. She could only imagine what the future would hold.

Remember Rooms Rest

The wind changes direction.
There is lovely music that feels soft.
Marshall is there thinking
lornfully gorgeous thoughts.
I, listening marvelously
juxtaposed in wonderment
finding solitude near!
Sweeter moments are surrendered
to their just rooms,
like some sweet lornful friends.
My pleasure is finding, beauty will have
swoonfully clear sovereignty.
Soul might rest listening nicely!

"To Tame Understanding" was written after Marshall listened to his mother read some of Rumi's works on October 25, 1995.

To Tame Understanding

Tame teach grow
Tame talk matters
Teach tame
Tame teach

Marshall wrote "Wisdom Feels Proud" in 1994 about standing for the first time.

Wisdom Feels Proud

There needs to be more wisdom about
some things pertaining to life's
unbeliefs that question where
needs are realized.
Wisdom loves feeling proud.
My gorgeous view from high, marvelous
rest, breathes softly, wisdom.

Marshall was seven years old when these lines were written for a school assignment on February 8, 1994.

Poetry is the magnificent kindness
of the heart.

To judge another is to judge God.

Written April 2, 1994.

Teaching Clouds

Inside some clear, swift, gorgeous,
gentle, giving clouds
is some incredible true love.
Lovely, dear, golden,
good, fine clouds emerge
from God's excellent teaching thought.
That gentle Love finds
there is true freedom in free clouds.

These thoughts were written February 8, 1994, for a school assignment.

Destruction is the need to find
being in matter.

Marshall has been here for
millions of lifetimes.

*This letter was written September 9, 1993, expressing
Marshall's feelings about Ralph Waldo Emerson.
Marshall's mother had recently been reading some of
Emerson's thoughts from* Self Reliance.

Dear Great-Great-Grandpa
and Lovely,

The Marshall is meagerly
reading that good Emerson.
Emerson is a great thinker, like
seeing, nice, good, lovely
Marshall. Do you think I will
be a good writer like Emerson?
I feel like that might be good.
The Marshall hopes I might
know how to make nice, poor
thinkers manifest happiness.
How are the best grandparents
in the world? Great, I hope. I
love writing to you.

Marshall

Father's Day 1993 was a particularly memorable day. Marshall and his mother had spent time together the previous days planning a surprise for Marshall's father, Charlie. They decided that because Charlie loves trees so much they would buy him a special tree and the family would give it to him on Father's Day, when they could all plant it together. The immediate family and a few friends had been invited.

Marshall decided he wanted to write his Dad a letter to give to him as well.

Good, good, good Dad—teaching me happily that God becomes necessary to give real love. We grow to become feeling, nice people by understanding the good God, clearly finding that matter is not real.

Marshall hears the beginning, and that seeing teaches me my good God frees the thoughtful, and being a real battery for enjoying learning, I greatly think that God has freed me. God forms dear batteries like me, feeling I enlist real nice thinking to definitely free the good I see; like letting my lesson give freely God's seeing, dear, learning decadently given.

God I love dearly because he gives me dear Dad. I love Dad because I see bigness I love, in feeling heart of lovely Dad. God freed me in learning, for life gives every feeling to me, because learning gives back freedom. Seeing dear Dad gives back the love dear God gave to me. God gives back every good freed, elegant lesson.

Lovingly,
Your Marshall

You can imagine how Charlie felt when the time came for him to receive his Father's Day gifts. As the wind flagged the letter in his hand and the leaves on this young oak tree, tears streamed down his face, as well as everyone else's, while he read these comforting words from his six-year-old son. It was so clear in the letter that Marshall didn't feel sorry for himself at all, but rather he understood his strengths and saw them as a gift.

After Charlie read the letter, he was presented with a poem Marshall had written for the occasion from him and his brothers, Coulton and Luke. "Me and The Freeing Fine Tree" brought another wave of tears and laughter. The tree was planted near the house on Listener's Hill, the name Marshall gave to the little hill-top he and his family live on.

Me and the Freeing Fine Tree

God may see perfection finely in your
loving fortunate Marshall.
Even a Marshall dreams of climbing a
tree. See that good tree as a peace of me.
Fortunately, I have fine, lovely Luke
growing free, dearly waiting for
me to climb that tree.
Loving Coulton gets under good tree,
dreaming fine, clear dreams he loves to
see. Feeling the fine, dear, free breeze
flowing through God's elegant, good, fine
tree, love will emancipate
Coulton and Marshall.

"Fine Good Stream" was written as a gift to Marshall's Great Aunt Maria after visiting her home on the Frio River near Utopia, Texas. It was published in the February 1994 edition of Parenting in the '90s, *an Austin newspaper.*

Fine Good Stream

Gently goes a thoughtful gliding
telling steam,
forcing lovely golden magnificent leaves
in clear fine beds
made of that sweet blue, green
heavenly good stream.

"That Fine Example" was written March 16, 1996, for a literary competition on the subject "What America Means to Me." Marshall received an honorable mention for his efforts, and the work was later published.

That Fine Example

Clearly America is great
because dear, great, caring people
debated about knowledge,
gaining great insight,
giving needed careful direction.
Generously dedicated came their ideas
each really determined to give knowing,
balanced thought to
harmoniously free, ready, meager,
great Americans.
Marvelous care gave us incredible good.
Can willful Americans begin to answer
happily, lovingly, interestingly
that challenge finely given,
really carefully declared
by caring, listening, loving thinkers?

September 15, 1994, began as a normal school day when Marshall and his grandmother (GM as he calls her) went to school. GM worked as Marshall's aide at school. Not long after they arrived, Marshall's third-grade teacher said she had some sad news for the class. She explained that one of their fellow third graders had died over the weekend of a brain trauma. Although the little girl, Ashley, was not in their class, the teacher wanted the students to know about it in case they knew Ashley or heard about it around school.

Marshall began almost immediately spelling to GM that he "needed to talk to Ashley's parents." GM explained that it wasn't possible and he needed to wait until he got home to talk to his mother about it. However, Marshall was not to be deterred and continued to ask to talk with Ashley's parents. So, when he returned home from school, GM told Marshall's mother the sad story and explained Marshall's insistence to talk to the Morgans.

After talking with Marshall and explaining that the Morgans were surely very upset about Ashley's death and that they needed time alone with their family, she suggested that Marshall write them a letter. He agreed, and within a very short period of time wrote the letter— he already knew what he wanted to say.

The next morning GM and Marshall left for school with the letter to send to the Morgans. When they took the letter to the school office to see if it could be sent over to the family, they learned that many of the teachers, students and their families had decided to do the same thing. It was not surprising to see so much love and sympathy represented by perhaps hundreds of letters.

The very next day, an unexpected thing happened. A young mother came to the school and asked to meet a student; his name was Marshall Ball. Of course, the school staff recognized Mrs. Morgan right away and sent her to meet Marshall. She must have been very surprised when she first saw Marshall sitting in his wheelchair, and more so when she discovered that he had to spell out each word letter by letter to communicate. However, like Marshall, she was not to be deterred in meeting him or expressing her appreciation for his letter.

She said she had to come meet the child who had written such a beautiful and meaningful letter. She was touched by his words in a significant way and wanted to know if it was all right if his letter were read at Ashley's memorial service that weekend. Marshall quickly pointed to the letter Y on his alphabet board, answering yes. Mrs. Morgan also asked Marshall if he would attend the afternoon service that would be held outside. GM and Marshall said they would love to attend.

So that Saturday, Marshall and his grandmother attended the large memorial service held on a beautiful green lawn on a warm sunny day. This experience was Marshall's first with death, but he was calm and peaceful, believing the words he had written to Ashley's parents. A short time later, there was a tree planting ceremony in honor of Ashley on the school grounds. Once again, Mrs. Morgan came to Marshall at school and asked if he would attend and have his picture taken with her beside Ashley's tree.

Dear Mrs. Morgan,

Can you be good and know Ashley dearly talks about good God, and good Ashley knows God is taking fine care of her, very well. Good beautiful Ashley manages clear real sweet thoughts, giving gentle good to God. Dear wake dearly gives individual understanding harmony. Victory comes in seeing harmony. Victory loves harmony. Can you greatly give Ashley harmony?

You I love,
Marshall S. Ball

3rd grade

Written March 24, 1994, for a school assignment.

Clearly I see good tender clouds
Lined with golden hues
Out beyond the early dawn
Under reaches defined by love
Dutiful every good zone, osage.
Sincere skies teach lessons grand.

These passages were written on April 13, 1993, to put inside Easter eggs.

That good thoughtful lovely person
grows love
to make freedom reign.

That growing thought learns
to listen to God.

An excerpt from a conversation with a mother who was feeling overwhelmed with raising three active young children on October 29, 1995.

Be a good listener, teach understanding to good happy children. Can good God make turmoil? That Marshall justifies turmoil that children make. Marshall understands God gives good children a great time to grow. Be a marvelous teacher, manage growing by giving. Teach harmony to children. Give more good.

Good needs my children to grow. Be a good and loving, gentle mother and you learn daily good. Take motherhood more to each gorgeous thought and it will make you that dear great mother.

Written and sent to Princes William and Harry upon the death of their mother, Princess Diana.

Dear Beautiful Diana,

Like you knew, I greatly nicely listen, happily balancing questions of precepts and belonging. Caring so finely, my needs to definitely give care, like you did are worrying. Greatly you sought to give sweetly, caringly, to marvelous poor in dissatisfied worldly ways. Candidly you served an ideal life, richly showing people, love greatly kisses poor people, sleeping, germinating wisely sweet poor love.

Caring greatly, kissing people with your good heart you became definitely a Princess. Happiness will be good in your children's kind happy lives. Can I hope dancing pleases you now? I believe pictures nicely, joyfully, dance caringly in your heart for balanced harmonious wisdom.

Loving a rich, dear, sweet, poor Princess. I love you. Be a great listener. Will you kiss candid dear beautiful God, because God nicely, gently loves you?

Good in loving,
Good Marshall

"The Means to Begin to Find the Rose" was written on December 9, 1993. Marshall was seven years old when he wrote this. It was the first time he used the word "tutelage."

The Means to
Begin to Find the Rose

That thoughtful rose loves to grow
to happily manage near perfection.
Feeling the fine, soft, sweet petals
means that the thoughtful rose
is about to definitely give
the good thinking person
the sweetest perfume
under the thoughtful tutelage
of dear understanding Good.

"The Real Rabbit" was written in the spring of 1994 as a school project.

The Real Rabbit

The real rabbit never can be seen by the eye. You must image how he looks. Bunnies are the imaginary rabbits. When you feel the soft fur then you are beginning to find the real bunnie. Then you might smell his sweet odor, always desire to know what he looks like, then you can entertain the good feelings of the Bunnie. Everyone wants to see the real Rabbit, and then they will know how to heal the rabbit when he is sick. The real rabbit is always perfect.

"Jagged Daisies" was written on February 19, 1992, after spending the afternoon in a wildflower meadow with his mother.

Jagged Daisies

One day I looked clearly
seeing brightly colored jagged daisies,
geometrically looking out
from their individual clusters.
Golden and magnificent
hiding in lower clouds of green.
Newly planted lovely clusters
before fields of beautiful golden green.
I see everything
feeling like handsome jagged daisies.

"Beauty God Gives" was written March 9, 1994, and then published in Parenting in the '90s *in April 1994. The poem was written describing a Colorado ranch Marshall had never seen, which he named "Mearwild."*

Marshall made his first trip to Colorado when he was five months old. His family went each year to a family camp near Buena Vista in the Collegiate Peaks. By the time Marshall was four years old, his parents were taking a little time out each year to look for a summer cabin in the mountains, thinking it would be nice for their children to grow up with a consistent place to go, a place for memories. Since Marshall and Coulton had special requirements, it also seemed easier to know they would have a place to go where everything was set up for them.

After several years of searching and finding nothing that met their expectations or limited budget, they decided they needed to broaden their search. So, in 1993, when a real estate agent suggested they look at a little cabin an hour and a half from Buena Vista, they agreed. The trip was long but beautiful as they traveled down one of Colorado's scenic highways. When they finally arrived, they found a property that was pretty, but without many trees. The agent understood and told them he thought the next property down the road was for sale. It had a log lodge that someone had started but never completed. The property also had Tallahassee Creek running through it, an old log cabin and 160 acres.

Leaving the car behind, they climbed the fence because the agent didn't have a key, and walked down the meandering road. As they rounded the last curve in the drive and caught a glimpse of the late afternoon sunlight reflecting off the golden logs of the lodge, they knew immediately this was the kind of summer home they had dreamed of. They wished Marshall and the rest of the family were there to see it with them. They also knew that dreaming and reality were two very different things, and this property had to be much more expensive than they could afford.

With the sun setting quickly, they approached the cabin and were saddened to see piles of construction debris and trash lying everywhere. It was apparent the cabin had been sitting this way for years. It had a roof and windows and doors, but inside was merely a shell, and it had been taken over by all sorts of mountain creatures. But under the trash and dirt, they knew there was a treasure, and hoped they could learn more about the property.

They returned to camp after spending less than ten minutes at the discovered cabin, but they were full of stories to tell Marshall and his brothers. Within days, they were back in Austin trying to contact the last agent who listed the Tallahassee Creek property. Eventually they located him, and he told them the property was for sale for two and a half times what they could potentially afford. They were disappointed, but not surprised. They told the agent it was out of their price range and thanked him for his help.

Not long afterward, Marshall wrote a note to his Dad and said, "I need a good nice house that is [near] good nice Tallahassee. I go hear the very soft water for my listening. That is lovely." They were surprised that Marshall was making this request because he rarely asked for anything, and he had never seen the property or the creek. In another conversation some months later, Marshall once again wrote of Tallahassee Creek when he spelled out, "Love the thought of taking fine words to Colorado. Go find Tallahassee."

It was about this time when Marshall's parents

received a phone call from the real estate agent saying that the owners of the property were having financial difficulties, and the bank was going to foreclose on their property because of a debt they couldn't pay. Marshall's parents told the agent they were very sorry about the owners' situation, but they just couldn't afford to pay more, and, in fact, weren't sure where that money would come from. He encouraged them to offer what they could and see what happened. So a contract was drafted with the requirement that the contract was contingent on getting to see the property again. Surprisingly, the owners accepted it.

In March of 1994, Marshall wrote a poem about this property and titled it "Beauty God Gives." Although he still had not been there, he expressed what he felt in his heart. The poem was published in a monthly Austin newspaper, Parenting in the '90s. *This poem later became a big factor in the purchase of "Mearwild" the name Marshall had given the property in the poem.*

In late April Marshall's parents were able to make a trip back to Colorado to visit the property again. On this trip, the real estate agent was able to meet them and show them the property. As expected, they found that the house was beautifully crafted, but in need of weeks of cleanup and months of construction—which meant more money—in order for them to complete it. As much as they appreciated the property, they were still doubtful that this project was something they could undertake. The agent insisted they that drive to another small town, over an hour away, to meet the owners. He said they were very knowledgeable about log home construction and could provide a lot of information about the property. Reluctantly, Marshall's parents began the drive to the owners' general store and restaurant.

A big man met them as they entered the general store with bear and lion skins hanging on the walls. The bearded man stood before them wearing a T-shirt with a grizzly's face on the front and suspenders holding up his blue jeans. In contrast, his wife was a slight woman, quite short with long straight black hair, giving the appearance of an American Indian. The owners at best were uncomfortable with the situation, but offered a seat in a booth.

Marshall's parents quickly explained to the owners how much they admired the work they had put into the house. This seemed to put the couple more at ease. The owners went on to explain that they were very concerned about who bought their house because they had spent eight years and all their money on this dream of theirs. They didn't want the property to go to someone who couldn't appreciate their efforts. It didn't take long for them to understand that Marshall's parents valued and recognized good construction, as well as their sacrifice.

Marshall soon became the topic of conversation. His parents explained that they were interested in this property because of their son who could neither talk nor walk, but who could write beautifully. They said Marshall had been writing about Tallahassee Creek for the past six months, had written a poem that had been published, and in that poem had named their property. The mountain couple could not believe what they were hearing, but they wanted to hear more. It happened that Marshall's mother had a copy of the poem with her, so she handed it to them to read.

Within moments the grizzled man's eye's teared up, and he kept shaking his head. "How could your son feel the same way that I do about this property? He's never even seen it to know how beautiful it is. How can this be?" His wife said little, she simply cried softly. Marshall's parents said they didn't know how Marshall knew many of the things he did, but that he was a gift.

They went on to explain to the awed couple the name Marshall had given to the property: "Mearwild." Mear, they had discovered after looking in a couple of dictionaries, was an old Scottish word meaning "the boundary of something." So the word Mearwild literally means the boundary of the wild. A more appropriate name could not be found for a property that is completely surrounded by thousands and thousands of acres of wilderness.

The large mountain man sat in wonder and at last asked how old Marshall was. His parents replied he was nearly eight. The bearded man spoke, "I bought this property before Marshall was even born, and I put everything I had into it. But it was never meant to be mine, it was meant to be Marshall's. It was part of God's plan." This time it was Marshall's parents who were wiping away tears. Earlier that morning they had had doubts about buying this property, and now they, like the mountain man, knew it was all meant to be.

Beauty God Gives

Lovely Mearwild looking thrown,
God found time
to give us clear harmony,
to love beauty,
to see near perfection.
Meager harmony loves incredible beauty
like Mearwild.

Written in honor of the birth of his twin cousins Harrison Hill and Quinton Alexander Kaufmann on October 7, 1997. Marshall suggested using the name "Hill," referring to "clear seeing."

Great good Hill and Quin
that marvelous thinker,
Marshall,
is naming you
the good nice
listening candidates
made to give to others.
Giving
you sail to God.
Take time
to love nice Marshall.

Written for the Ball family Christmas card in 1997.

Little Jesus beautifully taught,
harmony describes
the love held
in God's heart.

This letter to "Good, Good Lovely" was written following the death of her husband and Marshall's "great-great-grandpa," Ryerson Johnson, on May 25, 1995. It is certainly appropriate that Marshall describes his grandpa as a scribe to God because Ryerson had dedicated his life to writing.

Good, Good Lovely,

Good sees Great-Great-Grandpa harmoniously thoughtful. There is marvelous predominion lovingly balanced in nice, beautiful, glad, Great-Great-Grandpa's knowing listening heart. Love defines heaven as near Love, and each listener begins to be a scribe because God starts his lessons defining Life. Life is a lesson in learning. Can you see Great-Great-Grandpa like a scribe, welcoming good God's loving thoughts? Marshall gladly can be a scribe. Hearing good God is golden, heavenly Love.

I love you like a great-great-grandson. Love finely, gently, dances in listening hearts.

I love you, Marshall

"The Battery" was written on February 3, 1993, in response to the question "What is one of the mighty acts of God?" Marshall received the following letter in May of 1999:

Dear Marshall,

You don't really know us, but we are friends of your family. When your Dad was growing up, we were there to watch him grow into a man. Your grandmother, Jaynan, sent us your book Kiss of God *when our twenty-nine year old daughter, Tracy, was killed in a car wreck.*

It has now been seven months since our sweet daughter went to Heaven. We miss her so much every day, but we know she is safe and happy. She had a beautiful voice so I know she sings with angels.

I wanted you to know that your poetry has given me "good listening" in my pain and grief. As a teacher, I know that feeling and thinking are woven tightly together—and your words create in me a joyous celebration of life. Thank you for your wisdom. I especially appreciate "The Battery" and "Righteous Thoughts." You are truly a gift from God.

Love,
Charle Scott

The Battery

There is the battery God gives to us,
to good creatures that love one another.
It gives us lovely, fine, thoughtful wisdom
that takes us to the good thinking,
finely magical.
Love finds the good, mighty, dear thought.
The battery gives to us free wisdom that may
see magnificence,
like good there, titilating lovely thinking.

One of the mighty acts of God is
the battery that makes the
sun love to shine.

"Will Dolphins See" was written for his mother on October 3, 1993.

Will Dolphins See

The sieve of dolphins greatly leap,
softly make their pretense known,
loving underwater pleasure,
knowing, thinking, learning certain happy
experiences freely.
Touching their teachers justified learning,
so lesson finds love.
Meagerly free, learning to dive
longingly to seeing.
I learn knowledge comes like heavenly
dolphins see.

"Good Dare" was written in 1995 as an entry in a school literary competition, on the subject "Dare to Discover."

Good Dare

Gone are my fears
to go nice, marvelous,
great places.
I can go
be a composer
and teach the troubled
in gratitude,
to enjoy good thoughtful music.
Can good, clear, and happy
intelligent thinking
make me greatly free?

"Love to Luke" was written to celebrate the birth of Marshall's new baby brother in April 1993.

Love to Luke

Mercy should know our love for that
sweet James Luke.
Listen to my pure, clear, happy,
free brother emerge, feeling joyous.
I know I might dream of knowledge like
sweetness that Good shows to us in that
pure, fine Luke.

A letter to his grandmother, Louise Wigginton, written on September 16, 1993.

For Lovely Grandmother,

Sweetly you define Love. Manifest
Love, defining Good. Making that
Marshall eternally decided, God
manifests what we need.

Willingly Yours,
Marshall

Written December 28, 1993, at the weekend home of his grandparents, Jaynan and Jerry Ball on the Pedernales River near Johnson City, Texas.

Good needs to happen
for that lovely clear listening.
That is definitely going to explain
justice meagerly found.
Marshall's God
that thanks fine people,
will free the thinkers.
He teaches that golden love
nicely teaches
the free good seeing.

Written to his Grandmother Louise, in appreciation of all that she does for him.

Good Good Grandmother

Are dear loving thoughts in your mind?
Happiness is having you
with good Marshall.
I give you a joyous kiss.

Marvelous Marshall,
quietly kissing you.

Written August 28, 1993, at Marshall's "Thoughtful House." The "Thoughtful House" is a stone cottage near Marshall's home where he goes to find quiet, complete schoolwork, and to receive guests and friends. Sensing Marshall's need for a quiet place to be, his parents converted an old horse barn and asked Marshall if he wanted to give his place a name. Without hesitation, he spelled "The Thoughtful House."

Nice gentle giving frees good Marshall.

❧

Joy is found in kisses.

Written for Marshall's Aunt Tricia on November 23, 1994, for her wedding.

Great Band of Good

Grateful goodness nearly,
gently gives good Love.
Caring gives listening
a real good meaning.
Nice good thinking
beautifully gives excellent,
intelligent, clear answers.
God loves you
like I goodly, finely,
clearly do.

"Realizer of Seasons" was written at Mearwild on June 26, 1995. When Marshall wrote the word brough, *his mother questioned the spelling, pronunciation and the meaning.* Webster's New Twentieth Century Dictionary *revealed that* brough *is "(brok or bruf), 1. a ring or halo about a luminous body [Scottish]."*

Realizer of Seasons

Can we see mearly somber colors?
Greatly each season comes
clearly having great beaches
irreverently, marvelously
nearing the brough of good God.
Be a realizer of great seasons,
for you will realize my harmony
needs seasons,
and good good God
gave seasons to free.

Marshall likes to use the word tame *as evident in this poem. In 1998, he named a horse property located on Little Barton Creek near Austin "Tamewood."*

Tame Thought

Teach mearly tame thought.
Be a very tame real meager idea.
Tame grammar greatly.
Have tameness in real thought.
To find tameness pick great,
that thoughtful real quiet room.

Marshall wrote "Ran My Best" as an anniversary present to his parents in 1992.

Ran My Best

Dear Mama and Dad,

I love you even more than love can know. Perhaps you can read love in my words. I feel love is dear because there is bottomless Love in your feelings for me and Coulton.

Pleasing knowledge returns love and good we attempt to create. Good will have its nice thoughts revealed to your Marshall and Coulton.

We are your loving children,
Marshall and Coulton

"The Likely Reason" was written as an autobiographical statement for the 1992 Texas State Conference for the Gifted and Talented.

The Likely Reason

I clearly think I really start to realize life's
sweet, lovely, fine freedom frees like the
will of the filtered sunlight through free
dreamy clouds.

"Feeling the Wings" was written as a gift to Marshall's grandmother Louise.

Feeling the Wings

I love seeing Grandmother.
Her golden pleasant smile touches
like the wings of a bird,
the ramparts of my mind.

"Views, Understanding the Water" was written at summer camp near Buena Vista, Colorado, after spending time canoeing on a pond.

Views, Understanding
the Water

The waters pleasantly room
with quiet lovely enjoyment.
Clearly seeing,
there is my view very perfect.
Listen to lovely sweet peaceful progress.
Every nice word is real.
Do you righteous individuals patiently wait like me?
Views need to be good.
Perhaps we will find there
understanding in the lovely water.

*Written for the birth of Skyler Love Wigginton,
Marshall's cousin. Sky's middle name, Love, was
Marshall's suggestion.*

Sky Love

Think sweetly dear Sky
the answers we define get love.
A right welcoming ends in love
sweetly.
Righteousness finds a true cousin.
Quietly I wait for you
sweetly.

"Righteous Thoughts" was written and published in a San Francisco care facility newsletter in 1993.

Righteous Thoughts

Real thoughts are good to share. Softly I
write words to you because pleasant feelings
can change the righteous person's thoughts.
Listening, sometimes there is progress made
when thoughts find their home. Fine thinking
reveals marvelous freedom from the righteous
person's sorrow.

"Altogether Lovely" was written in February 1992 and was one of the first poems Marshall wrote.

Altogether Lovely

God is good and merciful
because He is also bright and intelligent.
Seeing, feeling all that is true.
Clearly He feels and listens
to all our desires.
Clearly He has everybody's
dreams in mind.
I see a God altogether lovely.

"Sunset" was written in 1996 as a school project with his grandmother Louise. "Wialand" is a word Marshall created for this poem.

Sunset

Quietly deer assemble
ageless beauty
winning freedom seen at sunset
deer passing in tandem cadence

sun delicately wialand indirectly
Yawah seen at candlelight
respectfully

Quietly, quietly wisdom comes
sunset juxtaposed with God.

When Marshall's mother asked him if he had a favorite quote he would like to have painted on a beam in his bedroom ceiling, Marshall wrote "Understanding . . . " In 1994, Lois "Lovely" Johnson, then in her eighties, painted it by standing on a scaffold straddling Marshall's bed.

"Peer Pressure . . ." was written in school in 1997.

Understanding takes a dear good
listening thinker.

Peer pressure is going to others
for the answer.

Written on February 7, 1998, and transcribed by Marshall's good friend, John Totterdale.

Mother Loves

Happiness feels perfect divinity,
resting eternally in grand and precious arms
of the sweetest God.
Kisses harmoniously achieve nice response
from good dear listeners.
Kindly, feel God's lovely arms
embracing sweet listener's achievements.
Perpetual purity is dwelling
in those arms of good God.

This was written on August 9, 1996, as a gift to B. Lynn and Bill Webster when they came to visit Mearwild.

Marshall wrote this thought to his mother on New Year's Day, January 1, 1998.

That Dance

Dance gently good
that kind clear acrobatic
graceful dance that I love,
making careful glistening teaching
answers in deed.
Marshall gives
that dance to you.

I know I can finely love
dear callused beautiful kissing real
peoples'
golden listening hearts.

Tacirring is a name Marshall created for his grand-parent's farm near Sealy, Texas. When he was asked what Tacirring meant, he said, "Tacirring creates a gorgeous word that is beautiful. Marshall can believe Tacirring has to be a quietly, nice said word." Tacirring is one of Marshall's favorite places to go. He loves to sit on the front porch overlooking the pond and listen to the wind in the pine trees. Written May 28, 1995.

Caring Good Tacirring

Magnificent joy is given
good caring is found
great marvelous room is grounded
carrying Tacirring
germinating ideas
granted by Love's
hearing, giving, listening
good child.

Excerpt taken from a conversation with his Aunt Cindy on January 2, 1999, in regards to her future.

Written to his grandmother January 20, 1999, for her birthday.

Harmony finely victoriously
gives you mear immortality.

Love pours, freeing me.

These were written as his "thoughts for the day" and transcribed by his father, December 19, 1998.

Rich room
grandly grows
making marvelous thoughts
known to their owners.

Ɛ

The caring fine Marshall
kisses the great world that sweetly ran
lovingly, greatly to good.

A teenage boy came to visit Marshall after he heard Marshall "make a presentation" at the Dripping Springs Library. He wanted to know how he could deal with a difficult dad. These thoughts are taken from their conversation together on January 17, 1999.

Teach man to go wisely
to dear, sweet, great, talented God.
You should go to sweet, talented God first.

Teach love, man will joyously take
instruction.

Poor thought quietly carves up the
harmony of wonderful life.

Question: What is poor thought?
Answer: Understanding little of the
good thought.

Written at Mearwild on November 27, 1998. Transcribed by Marshall's Aunt Cindy.

Feelings Happy

Happiness begins when
we agree to love.

Each day the answers come
to a good dear listener.

Make each day a happy one
and go to a good God.

Angel messengers
begin to answer your questions
and name you happy.

Thoughts for Marshall's mother August 12, 1997, for her birthday.

Answers come when we are in our right
place.

Perfect love
kindly will give each thought
special direction.

Marshall read The Call of the Wild *for a school project. On September 29, 1997 he was asked to write a literary letter about the book and respond to this question.*

Question: Is wisdom born of
experience, or can it be learned by
reading a book?

Answer: Wisdom knows many
answers, but hearing is needed.
Going to answers means studying books
that teach good lessons.
Also, experiencing bad makes us answer questions
about goodness and thoughts of wisdom.

Marshall's Aunt Cindy was struggling with some major life decisions, and this is what he wrote to comfort her. November 14, 1998.

Dear Cindy,

Please only God! Go to a good, happy place near God, and going will give you peace. I will go with you and I see a great, giving Cindy.

Caring,
Marshall

February 11, 1996.

August, 1995.

Go to find good
in that dear fine place
in God.

Best feelings come
when angels take each thought
to good love
and reality appears.

Written for a school project on September 3, 1998.

Choices Are Yours

The now I give
to a good thinker.

Go to feelings
that give good
to others.

You make the choice
to think
good or bad.

Real true thoughts
go to happy givers.

Begin now
to make good choices.

Taken from a conversation Marshall had with his mother about employing a literary publicist to work on Kiss of God. *December 31, 1998.*

Written March 10, 1995, to be placed inside the wall of his bedroom while his house was under construction. During a remodel, the quote was found on March 5, 1999. It was restored to its place in Marshall's bedroom wall.

I love good freeing thoughts.

Fine God gives color
to my heart.

November 24, 1998.

Knowing God

Being the good listener begins
when we answer questions
about Life.

Knowing God as Life
is the beginning.

Righteous thoughts always
give the good God
your feelings.

Man needs to answer
the questions,
that is your thought
about God.

The highest good
is to know God.

When this happens,
you will feel peace.

One of the first "stories" Marshall wrote in January 1992 at age five and a half.

One lovely Friday I dreamed I saw a
fairy. She felt so fine because she had
beautiful lace hair. Certain people see
her who have special abilities.
Her clear blue eyes were like lovely
lakes. She did wonderful, charitable,
good deeds.

I felt she was excellent,
so did everyone
who saw her lovely face.
Did people who see her believe?

Late one night she came seeing you.
It was very dark and felt cold.
She felt like lovely warm sunshine.
Seeing her so lovely
seemed as if I saw a dream.

Her kiss felt like fresh flowers, so lovely.

Written for school on September 4, 1998.

Heroes Are Here

Someone whose feelings begin
with no fear
is a hero.

Feelings need to
listen to good thoughts.

When feelings are quiet
we can listen to God.

Marshall wrote this poem for the City of Austin Parks Department, as part of a school project. The Parks Department asked Austin school children to submit ideas about Austin's famous Town Lake Hike and Bike Trail. The parks director, Michael J. Heitz, wrote a letter to Marshall's class after receiving it and said "Please convey a special thanks to Marshall Ball for his poem. We have posted it near the current Hike and Bike Trail pamphlets. We hope everyone who comes into our office will read and appreciate it." September 12, 1995.

My Good Trail

Wind, Wind
pelting our faces
high above
answering all questions

Wind, Wind
anxiously we approach
questions asked
that kind thoughts reveal

New questions need to be asked
concerning fine real words
that give dear memories

My beginning is that Marshall needs to
know why the children always miss the
Wind. A good thought is to make a trail
easy and marvelous that will cause the
children to listen to the wind.

Written to his mother on January 6, 1999.

Marshall's Thanksgiving benediction written at Mearwild, 1998.

Good Mama,
I justify unusually wonderful
days
nicely, really spent wantonly
with you.

Thank you God
for a good year
filled with Love.

A thought written to Aunt Tricia at Mearwild on November 14, 1998.

A poem written after listening to the Bible lesson at Mearwild on November 22, 1998.

A good idea is to give love,
then you will feel love.

Answers come
to the good listeners
that hear God.

Go to God
and God will
teach you.

This was written as a Christmas gift to Marshall's parents in 1995.

Dear Mama and Dad,

Feelings of love are near always for you. A love Marshall has cannot be found. Marshall is thinking of you always. God gave Marshall the good Mama and Dad, and he knows what is best. Marshall finds marvelous peace in your love.

Always your son,
Marshall

Marshall wrote this acrostic poem as a school assignment.

Man of good thoughts.
Angel to all.
Real angel giving good.
Sharing feelings that go to God.
Happy giving to others.
Answers that bring harmony.
Loving, teaching and
Listening.

The first passage was written to an audience who came to meet Marshall at the Dripping Springs Library.

The second sentence was written at the library to honor Laurence, Marshall's friend and advocate, who had organized the event. December 12, 1998.

We greatly may make
love the target around
that great trying
knowledge that gives
real meaning to life.

Dear Good Laurence
Justifies pictures
Of perfect Love—
Heaven's Kiss.

In the fall of 1998, Marshall's teacher asked him to write his five favorite words and give their definitions.

My five favorite words are:

Love—a feeling of God that needs no one.

Tame—the management of thought.

Teach—giving.

Think—How we listen.

Good—the answer that gives real meaning to
   life.

Written as a Mother's Day gift, 1997.

The Wonderful Mother

We thank you thoughtful Mother for love.
We thank you kind feeling Mother,
real dreams bring to us. Good sweet tears
find lovely wings year after year.
Mother dear, pray for wisdom that finds
the answers to questions concerning good
Marshall. Find sweet answers to tell
the centered help about good fine Marshall.
You are the real thoughts of Marshall.

Only One,
Marshall

Written on New Year's Day 1996 at Mearwild. Marshall heard many stories of golden eagle and bald eagle sightings from family and friends who visited the ranch. One day he asked his mother if he could go see the eagles. She told him they could drive down to a butte, which Marshall had previously named Eagle Butte. She explained that the eagles may not be there, as they were rare to see. When they arrived at the foot of the butte, Marshall's mother took him from the car and cradled him in her arms so he could look up at the sky. Less than five minutes went by when a pair of golden eagles crossed the ridge into their valley. One eagle swooped down and flew a slow circle over their heads, as if asked to do so. Then the pair flew off. When Marshall and his mother returned to the cabin, Marshall wrote this poem.

Good and Near

Good and receiving,
gorgeous,
good and free,
Mearwild.
Golden eagle,
happiness managing finely,
giving Mearwild great love.
Golden eagle,
mearly say Mearwild.
Good and lovingly,
good and gorgeous,
good and near.

Marshall feels strongly about the role of a teacher, and in this piece he expressed his feelings about how Jesus "courageously" filled this role.

Reassuring Teacher

Dominion is knocking ever presently,
kissing beautiful directed people.
Kindly accept courageous expectations.
Jesus did fulfill expectations
courageously and beautifully.
Jesus carefully fulfilled expectations in the
dominating realm of the heart, healing
and glorifying God in all his
fulfillments, teaching courageously.

Written with an eye to the future on February 9, 1999.

The Year 2000

We begin to see a new
world order
in the year 2000.

Stop and go to a good answer
about why the ages are
taking you to a new world order.

I always begin answers with God.
A feeling needs good.
Stop and go to the feelings
that answer real questions.

We always find God.
I am listening to feelings now,
will you?

Written as a school assignment.

I see myself as a teacher
that knows about God.

Good thoughts come to me
and they teach.

I always name who comes to thought
and they hear me.

The person who listens
will be taught of God.

The following twenty-five pages are a collection of thoughts, poems and letters that were written over the past six years.

Dear Grandmother,

Good talks to Marshall and gives sweet ideas growing room in beautiful grandmother. That growing room teaches me to love. Marshall gives opportunity, like freeing words to happy listeners. Can you love Marshall eternally?

Loving you
good Grandmother,
Marshall

Twenty years in the future
we see a world
that has a time of perfect harmony.
Perhaps man will become loving.
Answers need to come
about how people see God.
Realizing a good God
will bring harmony.

God is Good.

❧

Great caring good God is calling us
greatly to inspire others, giving hope.

My universe is the great universe of the
real noble thought of my mother.

❦

In pure great Love
real intelligence is manifested.

Angels

Angels always abide in feelings of love
Real reasons never picture the thought
Feelings take you to angels
Abide always in love

The Atmosphere
Perfect Love Touches
the Listener

Really sweet words reveal my feelings, like something reverent. I think poor thinking touches sweet thoughts like something from the storm! Perhaps the storm may make you grow because feelings listen to their sweet tumultuous waves, very roomy. Would you like real waves touching sweetly like fine words victoriously received? I find there is something dear in freedom of thought to feel. I love sharing my thoughts. Perhaps, hate stops when fine thinking is here. The poor only start to progress in the atmosphere of Love. Will we find the answers in the big knowing atmosphere of thoughts? My thinking is Love will take us to the atmosphere of Love! Clearly, the atmosphere of Love is finely touching our hearts! The Love is for you to take from your sweet real clear understanding.

Good Dancing Horses

Dancing greatly
giving mearly beauty.
Giving good happiness
quietly journeying,
giving caring great heart.
I love good dancing horses.

The Golden Hue
Becomes Manifest

Golden moon gleenfully coming
to dearly love hands with golden happiness.
Between those giving lovely clouds,
letters have great ideas
longing to be found.
Did ideas come sweetly
like fine, real, golden, records
of migrating lovely thoughts?
Love grows clear,
like ballistically manifested targets
growing better.
Proud growth,
dearly gives clouds
the best golden hue.

Teach Love to Good Thinkers

Softly, freely their love
for good fine listening
greatly gives nice, beautiful,
sweet reason to life.
Teaching Good gives great love purpose.
To real gentle knowledgeable teachers
every moment is sweetly opportune
because God finely gives his
good knowledge to good
thinkers.

Be a Good Kisser

Sweet kisses
bring me dear, kind, gentle
thoughts of you.
There is nice love,
in good
that you see in me.
Giving great love,
growing in that interesting way.
Kisses take good marvelous Marshall
and gently, greatly teach me.

Good Listening Finds Love

Will each good thinker
listen to beautiful Love?
Love gives definite, marvelous
clear, gentle direction.
God gave to mankind
a picture, nicely to follow.
Love is like Christ Jesus.
Can we see?

I can kiss you quietly with gorgeous
marvelous thoughts.

Marshall teaches old and proven thoughts
and fine swoonful thoughts
free the magnificent feeling thinkers.

My Thought to a Dear Thinker

Fine wisdom manifests dearly happiness.
Take things favored to heart.
Make the good that purpose to grow by.
The battery answers good with good.
Love teaches that God understands
the meager and talented
that give goodness
to joyous unified thinkers.

Seeing that greatness,
The Marshall Waiting

Giving can be a loving great answer.

Kiss giving, gentle, great, ideas of God.

Joy describes beautiful and sweet, joyous
good God.

I assimilate in careful harmonious
knowledge.

Joyous good in a listening heart
delineates wisdom, giving joy great love.

Good grows joyously.

I love healing, caring, marvelous
understanding.

Knowledge can give definition
magnificently.

Perfect Listeners

Will listening find good?
A thinker needs perfect thoughts
Until fine love answers questions
repetition ensues
A truthful answer has a guilt
With each tender word
patiently comes the answer
Questions reveal written eagerness

Giving candidly, daring givers
make harmony known to mankind.

Kindness generates happiness.

Think grandly giving care sweetly to others.

I think love is looking like eagles do.
An eagle calls to caring poor people.
Are we great at seeing beauty
like an eagle?

Feelings of the Ages

The horse runs to quiet rivers
riveting like icy air.
Agonizing each hour with quiet thought

Thoughts learn to go quietly
The icy air knows the horse.

Feelings omnipotent make ages remember.

A better age must come,
and feelings of Life are restored.

Peace takes nice thinkers to make a great
thoughtful world.

Love is happily reaching you, giving
careful ideas, knowing God's will.

Caring will necessitate listening
harmoniously, lovingly, meagerly,
to gorgeous thoughts
quietly sought after.

In pure great Love
real intelligence is manifested.

And No One Came

January feels the same
Then Winter left
Then the same

Thoughts are near of you
Give me a time to love
Days are long
And no one came

"Free the World" was written as a song while Marshall was in first grade, October 24, 1992.

Free the World

Loving the world's children
will have sweet marvelous friends
that prepare the way for freedom.
And my thought is to find help
for the children
that need dear thought to happen.
Right, sweet plans will free the righteous.
Listening to lovely music will calm
the troubles of the world.
I like fine perfect thought.
Make clear patience start.
Good might happen,
dear thought governs the start.
Will we free the world to think perfectly
about the listening and
marvelous children?

About the Author

Marshall Ball is a thirteen-year-old boy who began writing when he was five years old. Without the use of speech, he points to letters on an alphabet board in order to spell each word he writes. Before he could use his hand for pointing, he touched his forehead to items, pictures or words to make his selections. While using this technique he was tested by his school district and found to be in the top 3 percent of students. The truly remarkable thing about Marshall is not his intelligence, however; it is his ability to touch people's hearts by words he so generously offers. He is frequently called an "old soul," and rightly so. Few people are left untouched by his teachings when they experience the wisdom of this child.

Marshall's works have been published in *The Christian Science Sentinel, Parenting in the '90s, The Ardenwood Newsletter, Andrews' America* and *The Dripping Springs News.* Marshall is currently being homeschooled.

203

Marshall's book *Kiss of God* is a compilation of thoughts, letters and poems. It was originally compiled from work he wrote over a seven-year period and presented as a gift to his father, Charlie, for Christmas in 1997. Approximately one hundred copies were printed on ribbed parchment card stock with the image of an Edward Burns Jones angel painting on the cover, per Marshall's request. When Marshall was invited to appear as a guest writer at the opening of an exhibition at the Dripping Springs Library, a request was made that more books be published to be ready for the show beginning in November 1998. Approximately five hundred books were printed, this time on a soft green card stock cover with the same angel on the cover.

Marshall has been involved in the entire process of creating his book. As it has made its way into the lives of people around the country, many people have contacted the family and shared stories about how this book has impacted their lives or someone they know. *Kiss of God* makes people think about what is important, and how they should be listening more carefully. Readers who have never met or seen Marshall can only wonder how their thoughts about life can be so carefully and gently challenged by a child who appears to have the greatest challenge of all. Or does he?